Send Cardinals

Candidie

Archway Publishing books may be ordered through booksellers or by contacting:

Archway Publishing
1663 Liberty Drive
Bloomington, IN 47403
www.archwaypublishing.com
844-669-3957

Interior Image Credit: Candidie Lee Richardson

ISBN: 978-1-6657-1560-7 (sc)
ISBN: 978-1-6657-1561-4 (hc)
ISBN: 978-1-6657-1559-1 (e)

Print information available on the last page.

Archway Publishing rev. date: 12/07/2021

Dedicated to members of my family especially Tom, Tina, Elizabeth, Ellen and Carol who have convinced me to abandon my comfort zone.

Thanks to Gloria Bailey, Florence Fedeles, Barbara Taylor
and Robert Vanderpool for encouraging me. Hugs from now
'til forever.

Special Thanks

to

Julia Cameron

and

"Walking in this World"

These vignettes and illustrations are based on true events. Names, circumstances and descriptions have been altered.

Introduction

Some folks believe that cardinals are angels. Some folks say that's a myth.

I choose to believe that cardinals are sent by the Lord as a sign that one is being guided, protected and blessed.

Encounters with this beautiful bird come most often at a time of self-doubt and/or struggle. Having this creature in view allows one to be at peace.

Some folks say that angels are all around us. I'm one of those folks. I have seen them. When YOU do consider the spiritual grace their presence reflects, then look up to the heavens and say thank you.

Storyline

These four vignettes are character studies of couples who, in my estimation, need to reach out for spiritual sanctity to relieve themselves of their bittersweet loss of hope.

All four of these couples are baby boomers. Not that it has a decise relevance to the direction their lives have taken, but a sort of mirror image of practices, belief systems and problem solving abilities.

Having put these thoughts down on paper during the peak of the coronavirus in 2020, attitudes on my part and the parts of the characters may reflect on what it's like to be faced with a lethal pandemic no matter which way they've turned. Never has life seemed so precious, and never has time looked us in the eyes with such a threatening and foreboding force.

Yet, for those who are motivated by the need to help others in spite of the obstacles that crop up in their journey, the plight does not seem so overwhelming. We are here to do a job. He's got our backs.
Of that you can be sure.

"Come unto me, all ye that labour and are heavy laden, and
I will give you rest"
Matthew 11:28

The Family

Oliver the cat leaped off the porch and darted around the side of the house to the backyard. He was not fond of the mailman. The mailman always tried to give him doggy treats. He slipped into the shed where his master was busy working on a model ship and spread himself out beneath the wooden farm table.

On the back of the house was a deck, and on the deck was a dog. Actually, the dog was a part of Oliver's team of creatures; six dogs and five cats that would oversee everything on that property including the two humans who fed them twice a day. They made one happy family.

"Paws? Time for your medicine. I'll give you a snack," called the Mrs.

From out of the bushes there appeared a large, fluffy black cat. Before heading to the deck, he paused near the circular garden and sniffed at a wooden cross planted firmly into the ground near the rose bushes. Paws would always stop where Momo the kitten was buried. The cross in the dirt comforted the master and the Mrs. They were getting on in years, and it gave them a sense of hope.

Buddy the golden retriever rushed to where Paws lingered and chased the cat away from the garden. He had always loved Momo. They had played together into the wee hours of the mornings. The dog felt protective.

Paws took a detour to the feet of the Mrs. and let her give him his medicine, followed by a round, chicken flavored snack. Then he raced back into some bushes to hide.

Now Buddy was beside the cross in the garden. He laid with his big arms and legs sprawled out in the bed of violets. He knew that he was in a happy place.

The master stepped down from the shed and further into the house by way of the six wooden steps that led up to the back door. His lunch, prepared by the Mrs., was on the table. He sat down, and she joined him on the opposite side. Before they ate they prayed.

They prayed for their families. They prayed for their friends, and they prayed that the pandemic would end soon.

My main observation was that their health was failing. Yet, when they went out they wore their masks like a second skin. Both at seventy years old and burdened with so much debt that they drowned themselves in worry. They resorted to substance abuse as a way to escape their obligations, making their issues even worse.

She, out to save the world and he, confused as to what he should do with all the advisory comments directed towards himself. Also, he was supposed to be wearing hearing aids but mostly did not. There was well meaning moral support from both, but it usually fell to the wayside because both were stubborn as mules.

One was a vet, originally from the New England area, and the other a well bred Brit. Two regimented personalities exuding lifelong parliamentary behaviors. The control factor was remarkably evident in the woman with a lot of nagging and a sharp tongue. To defend himself the man would bicker right along with her like an old wash woman and later would fall into the depths of vertigo.

I wonder if they were specific in their prayers when reaching out to the Lord. Their repeated episodes of disagreement about this or that never resulted in any kind of smooth solution, and

now the restrictions set forth by the government kept them from having their own space. So, they wandered around blindly through their lives together biting their tongues and staying out of each others way.

They would sit in their den discussing each other's attitudes and behaviors while imbibing in their preferred self-medicating habits. A meeting of the minds as some would know it to be. Their cabinets and shelves surrounded them with relics from over 100 years past. Layer upon layer of dust filtered through the rays of sun shining from a western exposure. Their Christmas tree was a formidable impression of the real thing with an assortment of antiquated ornaments peeking through the dry branches. In most respects I would say they were holding on tightly to the past. And further, she tighter onto him than he to her.

The dogs slid in and out of the doggy door as did the cats who believed it was specifically constructed for them. In the summer the flower beds had no semblance of order or design. Simply planted, the flowers were put into the ground wherever there seemed to be an empty spot and in a sort of haphazard and wild array of color and species. It was impressionism at its best. But of course, these folks did nothing traditional and for that they were extremely proud.

So, where and how did their faith come into play? Especially now with nothing else for them to obtain some solace. Never speaking about the Lord, it was as if they lived their lives on a wing and a prayer. The name of the Lord taken in vain was apparent each time tempers flared about one thing or another. I did notice that the woman talked to herself, and loudly whenever she thought herself to be alone. Now when all is said and done talking to oneself is a ritual that does one more good than bad or so they say. Her rambling was curious and startling to behold to say the least.

Seemingly, they were both scouts at sometime in their lives as they would consciously and continuously do good deeds for others whenever possible. Bartering for favors was big on their list.

In all their daily scuffle their lives were becoming simpler. All was routine and all was habit. They moved slowly and pondered much. Their world lacked a fresh beginning. They married a long time ago. Never deviating from the familiar they've continued down the path laid out before them, never knowing what their fate was or when it was due.

Is it Hereditary?

There were only two places occupied on the long, tan sofa. She sat on the extreme end of the right side, and he sat on the opposite end of the left side; facing a television that was constantly blaring. This was the way life was these days. Everybody and their mother was under lock down.

On the end table next to her, was an overflowing ashtray. An example of the frustration and boredom she felt. In front of her was a coffee table with assorted bags of sweet and salty snacks. In front of him were his constant companions; his cell phone and his lap-top. Breaking news always appeared on the internet first.

It was evening and their nightly coffee dripped steadily into the pot as the aroma drifted into the living room.

There were no visible indications in or around their home suggesting faith, hope or any kind of belief system. Maybe they didn't feel it was necessary. Their bond had successfully brought them through many years and their strength came from each other and privately from the Lord.

They drank their caffeine and turned in.

Early the next morning their 40 yr. old son pulled into their driveway to surprise them. He actually didn't live far away, but they didn't see him much. He picked up a waxy, white bag of bakery from the back seat, put on his mask and presented it to his mom as he slid past her in the doorway. The two visited briefly in the kitchen before the dad entered in to share in the breakfast festivities.

The son wished them well a few minutes later and was out the door. The gold cross around his neck gleamed and flickered as it was caught by the rays of the sun.

He climbed into his van and headed to work. Being a chef at a local restaurant dictated that his hours sometimes included the first shift. They were only doing carry-out but his job was secure unlike so many businesses that were slowly sinking. Some days he would put in fourteen or so hours which didn't leave much time for his significant other and their baby girl.

His little girl actually went to a day care of sorts now taking only a few children at a time. Her mother worked as a housekeeper five days a week. The couple owned only one vehicle, the van. So the woman's mother would pick her up and then the child. Sometimes grandma brought along a casserole, a dessert or a couple of cheeseburgers for them, and of course, always something for her granddaughter. This particular day grandma brought the baby a solid gold angel pin for the child to wear on her shoulder.

"This will protect her," she urged as she attached the clasp to the baby's shirt.

Grandma departed and the child's mother immediately walked over to a wooden stand with three drawers. Laden with stress and worry she opened the top drawer, reached in and took out a joint. Not more than ten minutes after she lit up her partner arrived home. He entered the living room and stared at her with daggers in his eyes.

The baby giggled and cooed at the sight of her father. Her hand toying with the solid gold angel pinned to her pink t-shirt.

Dad's Kin

It was quiet. The lady of the house lay fast asleep in the large bedroom at the end of the hall. Her man, snoozing on the couch, was put to sleep by a re-run on the tube. In quarantine for the second week they had to stay home for a few more days. Having finished a huge meal of pork and sauerkraut they were both tired and took their daily afternoon snooze.

The man's cell phone rang.

"Hi Dad," he said in a groggy voice.

Dad, who lived seven hours away was in his ninety's and lived alone. The couple prayed daily for his well-being.

The lady, although past retirement age, was still in the workplace. Her husband had retired years before because of a disability.

Their surroundings were meager, yet the quality of their furnishings was well chosen. At the end of the hall, leading to the bedrooms hung an ornate, silver cross. It was encircled by family photos in silver frames.

The dryer buzzed loudly awakening the sleeping woman, and she methodically made her way to the laundry room. All a part of the routine.

Her husband, still awake from the startling phone call announced that his father had a serious case of Covid and was in the hospital. They knew that soon they would have to take a long trip.

Bringing the dried towels to the back of the house to fold she glanced up at the cross as she passed it and said a silent prayer.

The man got up from the couch and went to the kitchen. He reached into the fridge, took out a can of beer from the top shelf, and called to his wife.

"You want one?"

"Yeah," she called from the back room. Soon the towels were folded and put away into the closet. She joined her husband who was relaxing once again in front of the television and reached for her brew.

"We'll have to go up there," he said meaning Virginia.

"Maybe not," she assured him as she paged through her private phone book for the number of her father-in-law's pastor.

"If he passes, they won't let us have a normal funeral. He does have friends from the church ya' know?" she added.

"Fair weather friends." he said with disgust.

His wife knew well to what he was referring. The folks from the church responded to ailing fellow members if and when they had time in their "oh so busy" lives. Nobody wanted to take the responsibility if the inevitable were to occur. And now, so little could be accomplished.

The couple's father was bedridden. Alone and hooked up to multiple IV's his eyes were closed and he breathed heavily. Hours passed. Hours turned into days and days to weeks. After a three week period he fell asleep permanently.

Dad's kin loaded their car and drove the seven hour trip. When they arrived there was a lot of organizing to do, but with limitations on everything. The pastor came to visit, offered his condolences and gave a blessing.

All in all everyone did their share.

Two People

The birdhouse had three holes on each of the four sides. It stood on a ten-foot high, ten inch wide wooden pole. As the aging, dark skinned woman put out meal worms on the ledge of the porch for the chickadees, she explained that the bluebirds tended to inhabit the structure more than any other species.

As we visited together on the deck six feet apart, her disabled, Irish spouse sat inside with his recliner pushed all the way back. A football game was on the television screen. His life had been stricken with a rare disease a couple of years ago and there was an overwhelming, quiet aura of lost hope. A sadness in the air. The only reason their stone expressions changed from time to time was because of the antics of their cat who provided occasional entertainment.

Around the corner from the tv, high on a kitchen pantry shelf, rested a small prayer box. In the box was a pad of paper. Various hopes and dreams were written on the pages of the pad. It was a perfect place for the prayer box, as the kitchen was where it all happened. It was the room where the woman performed her wifely duties day after day.

At the end of the counter near the laundry room stood large cardboard containers of spices and seasonings for her home style cooking. On the window's ledge there were tiny bobble headed figurines put to life only when the sun came shining through. Her kitchen, her joy. The brand new flooring was the shade of caramel.

I left feeling as if I hadn't really been there at all. It was a sinking feeling in the pit of my stomach. As if I had been intruding. Yet, camaraderie was not happening anywhere to be found.

The next day was Sunday. The couple slept 'til noon.

So, what is the true definition of Sunday? The day of rest? The day to embark on absolutely nothing? The day to rejoice? Everything, even Sunday was out of whack.

The woman fed the cat, made coffee and picked up her cell phone. Limping through the hallway and into the living room the man landed in his recliner. Turning on the television and reaching out for the hot cup of coffee his wife served him, he found his favorite news network. 300,000 had died.

She got ready to go out, grabbed the keys to the Chevy, her leopard design mask and left saying she'd be right back. On her way out she watched her husband pouring whiskey into his coffee cup.

Their garden had failed that year; either from lack of funds or lack of tending. The cat had died. Their pick up broke down.

There was a snide, snappy tone in their voices when they spoke to each other, and to anybody else for that matter. Had they quieted and spoken to the man who could make a difference, perhaps their lives would have been easier, and then again, perhaps not.

They put up a for sale sign in their front yard one day with the hopes of changing their lives and moving on to a new start. However, isn't it true that we cannot change the world when we are unhappy, but changing ourselves may be the ticket. Vaccines became available a week later.

———◆———

"I will lift up mine eyes unto the hills from whence cometh my help."
Psalm 121:1

Printed in the United States
by Baker & Taylor Publisher Services